The Guy from Galilee

by

Amanda Baker

Copyright

Notes

All the pieces contained in this anthology are original and written by Amanda Baker. Some have been previously published in other works.

Editor – Dr EB Chaplin

Hand model – Mr J Crawford

Photo (pre cover design) - Ms K Lochrie

Contents

For my great grandmother Edna De Freitas

I was brought up and practiced as a Methodist for the majority of my life, attending Methodist Sunday School in Leamington Spa as a child and attending Methodist churches in a number of locations as I moved further North from Warwickshire in the shire counties of England to Edinburgh in Scotland via Northumberland.

I was lucky enough to head up a wonderful Sunday school at a church in Monkseaton. Much later and for some very happy years in Edinburgh I attended a URC church which I sadly left the year of writing this anthology. I have just started at a Church of Scotland congregation in the small village of Wallyford outside Edinburgh. But of all the different denominations I've attended there is only one writer of hymns that has me singing at the top of my voice without fail - Charles Wesley. If ever I am asked for a favourite hymn it would be this one and I even have a favourite line – 'my chains fell off'. This short opening piece attempts to explain what that line means to me.

'And can it be that I should gain

an interest in my saviour's blood'

'My chains fell off

My heart was free

I rose, went forth

And followed thee'

(Charles Wesley)

1.   My Chains Fell Off...

Doubt oppressed I barely breathed

Fearful lost and feeble

Hesitation all entwined

In the dark I lay confined

Cruel clasps around my mind

Until grace warmed me

Heavy yokes dissolved

My heart was liberated

And liberty was bound in You

Not in my scrambled self

My feet touched down

On steady ground

Tethers unwound

And now I'll try

To tread with purpose

On Your path

The essential story of the cross is impressed upon us relentlessly. Sometimes I think this is a difficulty when dealing with children. It's such a gruesome image it can be hard for a child to see past the physical to what it represents. At the same time, once we've grown up with this information it can lose its impact. And of course, to us puny humans with our disproportionate sense of importance, a couple of millennia seems a vast amount of time. In fact it is not much more than a yesterday.

2. On A Cross On A Hill In The Distance

On a cross on a hill in the distance

Woven through memory

A man cried out – *forgive them Lord*

Forgive them and take me

On a cross on a hill in the distance

When the world was fresh with wonder

A man was crowned with cruel thorns

Leaden skies were ripped asunder

On a cross on a hill in the distance

Glimpsed through centuries

We sense grey echoes of the crowds

As they fell to their knees

On a cross on a hill in the distance

Time sped on its way

Leaving a man bloody and parched

Renewed in us today

On a cross on a hill in the distance

That sacrifice was made

And for the sake of all mankind

The will of God obeyed...

In January 2023 the URC (United Reformed Church) I belonged to (but only really got to know properly after covid) put on a pantomime/nativity/family Christmas show; one I wrote following our work in children's church. Despite the lead dropping out due to a bout of covid the day before dress rehearsal, we managed the full run the first week of the New Year. It was fantastic fun. It was called *The Fed Up Christmas Fairy.* We had silly elves and a snooty narrator and a very snappy unhappy fairy who was missing the real meaning of Christmas. After all the fun and games and singing and slap-stick and bad Christmas cracker jokes, the angel came on to tell the actual story of Christmas in the neat package of a verse story.

3. The Angel's Story

A long time ago in a faraway place

A precious life was laid

On straw and wood for all to see

So human debt could be paid

Mysterious signs in deep vast skies

Brought strangers to Herod's door

Questing, searching and wondering

Astonished at what they saw

Close your eyes, be still inside

Listen to wisdom old

Every year in winter's dark

This gift of light will unfold

Lowly shepherds also gazed

Into that timeless firmament

Drawn by the power of unending love

To the Stable they also went

A promise was fulfilled that night

A child became the hope of all

Not in a palace jewel-adorned

But in a rough wooden stall

Close your eyes, be still inside

Listen to wisdom old

Every year in winter's dark

This gift of light will unfold

Whispers trickle down rivers and streams

As ancestors long gone

Relay the miracle told to them

That binds our lives to The One

Two thousand years tumbled away

And still we know this tale

And celebrate it every year

A joy that will never stale

Close your eyes, be still inside

Listen to wisdom old

Every year in winter's dark

This gift of light will unfold

Baubles symbolize the star

Presents mimic the tributes of kings

Little ones fill our hearts with joy

As like angels each child sings

So

Close your eyes be still inside

Listen to wisdom old

Every year in winter's dark

This gift of light will unfold…

One of the issues for folk who do not believe in God is lack of evidence. And while I see the evidence all around me I feel there are reasons we cannot know God in that sensory way that might satisfy some. Though I doubt they would be content because faith is never about that sort of proof. I'm sure Thomas would agree...

4. IF

If I glimpsed the whole

Even for a second

Glanced sideways

And perceived

All shades of love

And pain and joy

Hatred and redemption

Creation and destruction

If I caught a shifting shadow

Out of the corner

Of my eye

Slipping by

Guarding wonders

Soft cloud in front of sun

Muting the power

Of obliterating light

If I understood

Just a partial element

Of the whole

If I stumbled on the glory

My wretched flesh

Would dissolve

My retinas would burn

My mind implode

Merciful inadequacies

Shield me from

The wonder of God

Of course most churches get visiting minsters. And it can be a lucky dip...

5. The Minister Who Couldn't Sing

(or turn the mic off)

Oh dear – he realised - no control

Full voiced full flow

He was on a roll

Should he stop

He could not hold a basic tune

It was too late

And far too soon

The mic was on

The visiting minster stared in panic

Fumbled and searched

Increasingly manic

Where was the switch

Intros were done with amplified speech

But the mic off button

Was out of reach

And time to sing

And all we heard loud and clear

A booming drone

In everyone's ear

Above the throng

Even above his sonorous wife

Who belted out

For all her life

The correct notes

We tried so hard not to smirk

The minister had kindly

Visited our kirk*

Must be polite

But by a mile he missed each note

And bellowed on

Like an injured goat

My shoulders heaved

Please let it end please let it cease

Let us have quiet

Let us have peace

OR let us chuckle

A loud guffaw would surely help

But I fear if I do

It will come out a yelp

And offend

At last it's done the hymn is through

You dare not look at me

I dare not look at you.

But I reckon God is up in heaven

Laughing his socks off...

*Kirk is the Scottish word for Church

It goes without saying – the feeling of being alone is not necessarily about a physical state. I think most of us have felt it at the oddest moments.

6. Alone

Alone I am

Alone I stand

But when I open up my hand

I find a gift

Alone I am

Alone I lay

But when I face each testing day

There's fortitude

Alone I am

Alone I walk

But when I reach the dirt road's fork

There is a sign

Alone I am

Alone I fear

For all I love and all held dear

I plead a prayer

Alone, alone

In stifling dark

No scent of flower no trill of lark

Where is the light

Yet I am part of all there is

That's endless in the universe

I just need to reach out and touch

The Everything

Alone I was

Infinitely

But then I felt Him next to me

And knew God's grace

3... Truly I tell you, unless you change and become like children, you will never enter the kingdom of heaven. 4Whoever becomes humble like this child is the greatest in the kingdom of heaven. 5Whoever welcomes one such child in my name welcomes me.

Mathew 18: 3 – 5

7. When I Was A child

When I was a child

You guided me

You led the way

I trod the path

Obediently

When I was a child

When I was a child

You spoke to me

I heard your voice

I followed sure

Unquestioningly

When I was a child

Now I am grown

Lord guide me still

Lord speak to me

I'll walk your way

Unendingly

It was my Great grandmother Edna De Freitas who first showed me real faith (as opposed to 'religion'). Quite simply I could see it in her face. She was a member of a Caribbean 7th Day Adventist church which she used to take us to – my brother and me – when we were very young. At night she taught us to pray. Edna, who became the 'mother' of her church, was such a powerful sayer of prayers that people used to call at the house to ask her to pray for them. *Gentle Jesus Meek & Mild* was one I remember and which we said often at bedtime. As an adult, while I still love this prayer, I no longer think of Jesus as either meek or mild...

8. Gentle Jesus Meek & Mild?

Gentle Jesus meek and mild

Bedevilled in the desert

Tempted taunted

Options flaunted

Undefeated

Gentle Jesus meek and mild

Stalls tainting halls of worship

Toppled tables

Trinkets smashed

Overwhelming

Gentle Jesus meek and mild

Spoke truth to power

Taught in temples

Rules re-written

New foundations

Gentle Jesus Meek and mild

Full cup of sorrow

Tied and tortured

Saviour then

Now and tomorrow

And forever

Amen

I've mentioned attending church with my great grandmother; it was in Birmingham, home to an established Caribbean community. One of the things that struck me, back in the late 1960s/ early 70s was that the only white face I saw there was the pale, blue-eyed imagery of Jesus with gold ringlets. As a child it seemed odd to me. As an adult I find it hilarious that a Palestinian Jew should be still portrayed this way in our 'modern' world.

The piece that follows is a very old performance poem which I've entertained with at festivals and poetry events and even comedy clubs. You need to imagine the character parts in a Caribbean accent…

9. Shirley Temple Jesus

Three wise men came from afar

And got an awful shock

When they stepped into the stable

Avoiding cowpats and livestock

'Oh my lord, we spent too long

Staring at the sky

Or the camel got de hump

Or we just a bit high

Somethin' fishy goin' on
Something wrong – me tink
He can't be de saviour
He skin is far too pink

Who is it he look like ne?
Wit dat complexion and blondey curl
I know – I got it
Is dat Shirley Temple girl'

The wise men were amazed
When they looked into the manger
'Who de roots is dis
Milky Caucasian stranger?

Bruda Richardson tell Sister Stevens
Bruda Leroy give us a hincorrect route
Dis Baby is de wrong one
Even do he kind of cute

We need a map not a star
We'll do it ourselves and keep schtum

If we mark de destination wit a 'X'

We may find a bruda like Malcolm

Or Nelson or Tutu

Or bruda Usain

... Morgan Freeman could play all o' dem

Tuuut – we getting lost again'

They gazed upon the squidgey babe

In his swaddling nappy

Eyes as blue as fairy lights

They got irritated and snappy

'When we wend our weary way

And de journey finally stop

We dooon't hexpect a rendition of

De Good Ship Lollipop

We takin' back de presents nuh – WE LEAVIN.

Put everytin' in de sack

We goin' in search of de REAL Jesus

De one who's a little bit BLACK

I think this next piece is self-explanatory. I'm often shocked – when I shouldn't be – at the vileness some people seem to be able to extract from The Bible. I do wonder if they realise that what you see and receive can depend on the eyes and heart of the reader?

10. The Bigot & The Bible

Like a wolf in sheep's clothing

Though he doesn't know the word of the lamb

He wraps himself in The Bible

The Bigot knows his mind

He is proud of his prejudice

He winds himself in The Word

He does not hear the shepherd

Calling all towards him

In togetherness and safety

He casts the first stone

And the second and keeps throwing

There are not enough rocks

Where does he find them

As he injures those deemed lesser

Than himself. So many

He claims to know what's right

And right is on his side as

He aims and maims and wounds

Not for him the wounds that count

Just spite and derogation

As he faults all but himself

He despises 'them' in the name

Of Christianity

Clear profanity

The bigot sees his bigotry

Reflected in the bible

For him it is just a broken mirror...

Had to have a haiku...

11. Exposed

Exposed, faults laid bare

Unashamed before the world

Cleansed by forgiveness

Humans have complained about the biblical time span allotted to them. Apart from the most desperate and despairing, three score and ten years has seemed far too short and yet, compared to most of our animal fellow travellers in this world we have relatively long lives. Yes, this varies if we are lucky enough to live in wealthy countries with good health systems. Longevity disparities remain one of the key indicators of unfairness when we look at the effects of poverty v wealth in this imbalanced world.

Some folk, like my own grandmothers (on both sides of the family) managed to live well past the allotted time span despite a list of ailments and infirmities that would leave your family doctor needing lie down. This is about my mother's mother who was lucky enough to become a great, great, grandmother before she died.

For the purposes of this piece you need to know that 'stetic' was GG Olga's word for looking spectacularly well put together.

12. Death v GG Olga

'Let's go you've had more than

Your three score years and ten'

But Olga is not ready

She's on the phone again.

We tried to make him see

She's from the Caribbean

If you say be ready by eleven

She won't know what you mean

Ready by eleven means that

Sometime after two

She'll be looking for a certain blouse

And won't have found her shoe

Death muttered to himself

'Mrs Crawford won't play ball

That woman's never ready

No matter when I call'

'An extra quarter century plus

Is me just being nice

Surely that is time enough

To cook up peas an' rice'

All surfaces must have been bleached

Every catalogue perused

St Peter's grown impatient

The angels are bemused

No

She's still ringing friends or planning

Another birthday do

And even with just one leg left

She still can't find that shoe

Then Death got smart, turned up one day

Stetic top to toe

And Olga said

'Alright, alright

C'mon man let's go'

At the same URC church where we did the panto, there were other regular events for local families including the very popular holiday club. For 2023 the theme was The Circus. The children worked on ideas of personal value and that they all had something special to bring to the world.

In this story, the circus represents the material world though that will have gone over the heads of some of the children. There were fun actions to go with the repeated refrain. I've not listed them here as I'm sure you can make up better ones yourself.

13. When The Circus Came To Town

When the circus came to town

There was a jolly juggler

A smart ring master

A spangled girl on a high trapeze

A tumbling acrobat

A lumbering elephant

And a funny clown

When the circus came to town

The big top smelled of candy floss

As the people crowded under

The children laughed and the grown-ups clapped

And the brass band sounded like thunder

There was a jolly juggler

A smart ring master

A spangled girl on a high trapeze

A tumbling acrobat

A lumbering elephant

And a funny clown

When the circus came to town

There were stalls with bright toys

Roll up and win a prize

A strongman raised iron weights

I couldn't believe my eyes

There was a jolly juggler

A smart ring master

A spangled girl on a high trapeze

A tumbling acrobat

A lumbering elephant

And a funny clown

When the circus came to town

But when Jesus came to be with us

There was dust upon his hem

At first the crowds barely noticed

As he walked quietly with them

There was no jolly juggler

Or smart ring master

No spangled girl on a high trapeze

No tumbling acrobat

Or lumbering elephant

Or a funny clown

When Jesus came to town

There were miracles and wonders

And walking on water

There was bread and there was life

For each son and each daughter

There was no jolly juggler

Or smart ring master

No spangled girl on a high trapeze

No tumbling acrobat

Or lumbering elephant

Or a funny clown

When Jesus came to town

Jesus the Nazarene

The guy from Galilee

Suffered in this earthly world

Lived and died to set us free

When the marquee is folded

The tightrope taken down

When the trapeze is gone

With the jugglers and the clown

When the band is in the distance

And the crowds have dispersed

Then the first shall be the last

And the last shall be the first

The juggler has gone

The spangled girl is far away

Vanished like the acrobat

With the elephant old and grey

Gone too, the faded clown

They have all left town

Unlike the dazzling circus

He will not fade away

Jesus lived among us

He is with us today

There was a jolly juggler

A smart ring master

A spangled girl on a high trapeze

A tumbling acrobat

A lumbering elephant

And a funny clown

When the circus came to town

This piece was written on receiving the painful news that a loved, long term and much relied upon friend had been diagnosed with stage 3 lung cancer, wreaking terminal havoc in an already fragile body.

14. No Longer Contained

Contained in human form so strange

So delicate

Bending further to the ground

Your smile unchanged

My friend

Fragile flower of enormous power

Friend

You gifted wisdom

You gave me love

Gentle friend

The flesh betrays you painfully

My friend

And you must leave me

Devastated

My dear

The unchanging part of you

Dear heart

Will have no conduit I can use

I dread

Poor fool I am I need the 'you'

The shape

That I can see and touch and hear

Don't go

But these containers let us down

Frail vessels

The essence in us will be free

Released

All my fear and wanting cannot

Keep you

Precious unique irreplaceable

Leaving

And where you go I will also

Join you

My own container will reduce

To dust

This is the only certainty

Dear friend

We all will join The Everything

In the end

While I think of this as a 'secular prayer' it came to me on a Shrove Tuesday many years ago as I was heading home on the train with the day's news dragging me down. I arrived home to find my middle daughter making pancakes with my youngest daughter and the house filled with laughter and wonderful aromas.

15. Make Pancakes Not War

Make pancakes not war

Fall in love don't fight

Talk it over have a cuppa

Be filled with delight

Don't shoot to kill, plant sunflowers

Grow crops, fix the world

We can't call back harsh words

Once they've been hurled

Make peace with joyful noise

Have a hug be my friend

Don't go on like this

Stumbling to the end

Let the sum of your happiness

Outweigh your despair

Make pancakes *and* peace

If you dare...

The idea for this short poem came to me when I was in church – a rather patched together joint service which was nevertheless very good but my concentration was wavering. I was extremely tired and into the start of the 3rd month of a full-on house renovation. It was the most extreme renovation I'd done since my mid-30s and energy levels were taking a hammering.

Very aware that notes needed to be made whenever something occurred, I suddenly thought of the missing hand rail on the broken stair case and made a quick note.

This prayer floated into view.

16. When I Flounder

When I flounder fail fall please hold me

When I stumble stall struggle please help me

When I'm lonely lost loveless please find me

When I'm wakeful weary wired please calm me

When I'm needy negative neurotic please steady me

When I am groping in the dark be the lamp that shines.

And – yup – the bible can be confusing and a bit bonkers in places. Get over it.

17. So Much Begetting…

There's so much begetting

I keep on forgetting

Who is related to whom

Isaac wed his cousin

Joe had bros by the dozen

Joseph A owned Jesus' tomb

There's so much begetting

Some characters need vetting

Was Abraham's wife really that age

When Isaac came about

She must have been worn out

We need the advice of a sage

So much begetting

Misperceptions set in

It just goes on and on and on and on

Salome was related

To Mary who was sainted

And Zebedee was patriarch of John

So much begetting

It's all got me to fretting

The bible is bursting with babies

From Eden to The Fall

And Peter who was Saul

It's a jumbled pile of ifs buts and maybes

But in family spaghetti

Just don't forgetti

The wonder of The One who reigns above

All you really need

Is the very simple creed

The bit that says that - God is Love

I had thought to write a new piece concerning our failure of duty and careless attitude to this amazing planet but this remains a favourite of mine so I'll let it do the talking.

18. Does The Sun Still Shine*

Does the sun still shine

Do rivers still dance

Do breezes caress the trees

Does an apple still blush on a branch somewhere

Do flowers still flirt with bees

Does a waterfall crash where nobody hears

Does the Okavango delta still wash with Africa's tears

Do elephant bones lie bleached and broken

Are shorelines kissed by the sea

Are dead cities shadowed with ghosts and regret

The great whales just a memory

Is there a footprint left by me

Does a white moon glow where nobody sees

Could cathedral sunsets still bring me to my knees

Does the kestrel cruise with a predator's grace

While a vole marks his shadow, beware

Are the turrets and towers toppled and gone

Are the Great Plains stripped and bare

Is there anything there

Does rippling heat flatten the desert dust

Where scorpions arch and cacti pose and camels have
wanderlust

Are mountains still dappled by giddy cloud

Is my memory only a dusty store

Pale pretty pictures of paradise

Images of things that are no more

An empty room without a door

Our plundering and ravaging bore malformed fruit

Are the oceans and skies forlorn are forests blind and mute

Or

Does the sun still shine

Do rivers still dance

Do breezes caress the trees

Does an apple still blush on a branch somewhere

Do flowers still flirt with bees

Does a waterfall crash where nobody hears

Does the Okavango delta still wash with Africa's tears

* This piece appears in two previous works. *Zero One Zero Two* is a dystopian novella of mine where the forward narrative is in prose and the reflective pieces of the story are in the form of poetry. It is also in *Summer Anywhere* published by Hybriddriech, Edinburgh.

And of course there is the guy himself who we think of
and talk about after more than 2,000 years.

19. There Was A Guy From Galilee

There was a guy from Galilee whose feet pressed on this
earth

Before him kings and carpenters were equal in their worth

There was a guy from Galilee who came to share our strife

And to show us that he is the way the truth and the life

There was a guy from Galilee who lived the love he bore

When raging waters breach their banks, step out He is the
shore

There was a guy from Galilee the prophets had foretold

For thirty bits of silver this priceless gift was sold

There was a guy from Galilee who died upon a cross

His death was our gain our rescue, our freedom... not our loss

There was a guy from Galilee who taught upon a hill

And in a temple and by a lake, his footprints are there still.

There was a guy from Galilee

And we end of course with a blessing. Simple is usually best in my view.

20. Bless This Day

Bless this day

Guide our way

Lord help us

Bless my friend

Friend my foe

Lord teach us

Bless my neighbour

Bless each stranger

Lord we pray

My Churches

<u>Warwick Methodist Church</u> – Warwick
I was baptized here. My godparents still live in Warwick.

<u>Radford Road Methodist Church</u> - Leamington Spa
I attended Sunday school here and had a wonderful
Sunday school teacher called Miss Turrel. It is now a joint
Methodist / URC.

<u>Camp Hill Seventh Day Adventist Church</u> - Birmingham
This is the church I attended with my Great Grandmother
'Aunt Edna' whenever I was staying at my grandmother's
house in Olton. Initially the Caribbean congregation used
the old Church of England building but now have their
own smart building.

<u>Brunswick Methodist Church</u> – Newcastle upon Tyne
On moving to Newcastle to study English Literature &
European History (and later Law) I first attended this
Church – hidden behind the shopping centre.

<u>Jesmond Methodist Church</u> – Newcastle
Once I moved out of halls to a student flat, I attended
Jesmond Methodist Church but was later married out of
<u>Gosforth Methodist Church</u> as the church in Jesmond was
too small

<u>Westerhope Methodist Church</u> – Newcastle
My first and second houses after getting married were in
Westerhope where I attended and helped out with Sunday
school and where the then minister's lovely daughter
Claire helped me with childcare.

<u>Monkseaton Methodist Church</u> – Monkseaton, Tyne & Wear

On moving to the coast and after a brief stint at <u>Benton Methodist Church</u> (in-between houses) I attended Monkseaton Methodists. It was here that I ran the Sunday school for 7 years having begun on the very same day as the new minister Rvd Sharron Whittaker*.

<u>The Fisherman's Mission Methodist Church</u> – Whitley Bay

I briefly attended The Fisherman's Mission where a young minister and his wife were very kind to me during my marriage break up.

<u>Morpeth Methodist Church</u> – Northumberland

I attended the Methodist church here for a decade and was fortunate enough to encounter and fundraise for the Ugandan Pearl of Africa children's choir.

<u>Central Edinburgh Methodist Church</u> – Edinburgh

On moving to Edinburgh I attended Central Edinburgh Methodist Church where I was again lucky enough to work with the children and young people.

<u>Saughtonhall United Reformed Church</u> – Edinburgh

This ministry filled me with renewed faith and commitment. It was here I became involved in messy church, holiday club and other fun activities. When I first joined, there was no regular minister and talk of the church closing. It is now led by Rvd David Scott*.

<u>Tranent & Cockenzie Methodist Church</u> - Cockenzie
I now live in Wallyford and, having tried a couple of
churches, I find myself back in the arms of Methodism.
T&C Methodist is a tiny, pretty church with a friendly big-
hearted congregation and with a Welsh minister whose
voice is clearly made for the Welsh hills.

This is not a definitive list of all the churches or
denominations I've visited as I often like to call into
churches if I'm somewhere new or visiting friends and
family.

*Ministers whose comments appear on the back of this
book.

Also by Amanda Baker

<u>Adult novels</u>

The Companion Contract

Eating the Vinyl

<u>Dystopian novella</u>

Zero One Zero Two

<u>Epic environmental poetry story</u>

Casey & the Surfmen

(also available as an audio story on bandcamp)

<u>Adventure trilogy (8 – 12yrs)</u>

bk1. *Eleanor & Dread Mortensa*

bk2. *Eleanor the Dragon Witch & the Time Twisting Mirror*

bk3. *Eleanor & the Dragon Runt*

Picture book in verse for little readers

Ella & the Knot Fairies

Sort of autobiography

Maybe I'm not a Pigeon

Anthologies that include Amanda's work

The Iron book of New Humorous Verse (Iron Press)

ROOT anthology of short stories (Iron Press)

Lockdown Anthology (Scriptstuff)

Summer Anywhere (Hybriddreich)

Printed in Great Britain
by Amazon